beautiful DANGER

101 great road racing photographs

STEPHEN DAVISON

Pacemaker Press International

BELFAST

THE
BLACKSTAFF
PRESS

BELFAST

reaching for tar

Almost thirty years ago my father bought me my first motorbike, a gleaming Yamaha FS1E moped, or as they were better known, a 'Fizzy'. Although I was totally enamoured with my new steed, there was something else I noticed on the wall of the shop, an incredible picture of Raymond McCullough cranked over at an impossible angle going around Tournagrough bend at Dundrod. Two things followed; I spent a lot of time crashing and repairing the Fizzy, trying to emulate the angle of lean in the picture, and my interest in photographs of racing motorbikes began to grow.

That picture came back into my mind one evening in the winter of 2002 when I was completing the selection of images for an exhibition of road racing photographs called 'Beautiful Danger' at the Ulster Folk and Transport Museum. I wanted to include the McCullough picture in the exhibition; it was the benchmark against which everything else should be set. I had never met its author, Billy Reid, but I tracked him down to a little terrace house in Cullybackey village, County Antrim, and he was delighted to supply a print for the show.

That meeting provided the genesis for this book. Seeing my interest, Billy threw open his files of negatives and it quickly became obvious that he had a unique and largely unpublished array of pictures from the heyday of road racing, the 1970s. Set alongside my own pictures of the sport, we had the basis for this collection.

beautiful DANGER

101 great road racing photographs

Bruce Anstey at Guthrie's bends,
Isle of Man TT, 2002

The gaps were filled with photographs from the archives of Clifford McLean and Rowland White, men who have forgotten more about motorbike racing than I will ever know. Other eminent photographers, Derek McIntyre, Gavan Caldwell, John McIlwaine and Dave Purves, have also raided their attics and helped create this special photographic insight into the road racing scene over the last thirty years. As photographers, we have all brought our passion for the sport to the paddocks and hedgerows and a determination to highlight the sheer spectacle of road racing through our lenses.

It is the spectacle and tradition of this great sport and its heroes that are celebrated in the following pages. From its inception until the 1960s, when the first pictures in this book were taken, many motorcycle races took place on closed public roads. With safety and commercial considerations coming to the fore in the 1970s, the world championship Grand Prix events switched to purpose-built racetracks. The giants of the sport at that time, Hailwood and Agostini, are captured here gracing the roads for the final time. Their demise allowed a new generation of local road racers such as Joey Dunlop to have their day in the sun in front of the huge crowds that lined the courses in those years.

Today, pure road racing is largely confined to this part of the world. The Ulster Grand Prix, the North West 200 and the Isle of Man TT make up the blue riband events in the international motorcycle road racing calendar and are the setting for most of the photographs in this book. Alongside the national meetings held at tiny places like Killalane and Kells, Darver and Dundrod, these events offer a unique backdrop for the exploits of the new heroes.

Hunched behind the screen, David Jefferies hurtles between the hawthorns at the 1999 Ulster Grand Prix.

STEPHEN DAVISON

Hands of a champion

Brian Reid, Formula Two world champion, 1985 and 1986

Unlike most modern sportsmen, for whom the risks are nothing like as great, the men who race these courses are largely amateurs, riding for the fun of it. Affable and approachable characters who don't hide away from our cameras, they are happy to chat and share a drink in the beer tent after the event. Ever mindful of the risks they pit their skills against, the men who choose to race on the roads know better than anyone that this game is no stranger to tragedy. The litany of men who have paid the ultimate price for their sport is long and well known. There is no denying the danger.

But neither should we forget the beauty. It is this that draws us back time and time again to lie in the hedges, listening to the gathering roar that drowns out every sound and sucks the air from the sky. Our tea flasks drained and the sandwiches in the biscuit tin set aside, we wait for the first sight of sunshine glinting on helmets. They burst into view, tortured tyres dancing over the road, reaching for tar. The screaming blur of colour and sound, only inches from our faces, the waft of their warm breeze on our cheeks. Who was in the lead, who was second we shout – far too fast to take in. Then they are gone, off on another furious lap, only the shimmer of hot speed left hanging over the summer road.

Man and machine at incredible speed through the lanes and byways we travel on every other day of the year. Our roads, our heroes, our sport.

STEPHEN DAVISON
AUGUST 2003

7

on the edge
then . . . .

This photograph is a wonderful
rendition of man and racing machine.
The incredible angle of lean (on
skinny-ribbed tyres!) and the intense
concentration are caught in a perfect
harmony of speed and precision.

Raymond McCullough, Ulster Grand Prix, 1976   9

More than twenty years after Billy Reid captured Raymond McCullough at his stylish best, I lay in the same hole in the hedge at Tournagrough bend, Dundrod, and poked my lens through the grass to shoot Ryan Farquhar. A truly terrifying place, the riders skim around the corner on the very edge of adhesion, level with your eye.

The advance of technology in that time has given us better cameras and stickier tyres but the essence of both disciplines remains the same. As the racer takes it to the limit, the photographer tries to press the button at that precise moment.

A beautiful danger captured.

. . . and now

Ryan Farquhar, Ulster Grand Prix, 2002

agostini *italian style*

Incredible as it may now seem,
Dundrod's Ulster Grand Prix was one of the
rounds of the Grand Prix world championship
less than thirty years ago. Imagine Valentino
Rossi and Max Biaggi dicing through Jordan's
Cross and hammering into
Wheeler's bend on the
V5 Hondas today!

13

But one Italian of greater fame and reputation did grace these shores in those final championship years, the most successful racing motorcyclist of all time, fifteen times world champion, Giacomo Agostini.

Impossibly handsome and dripping with Latin flair and style, Agostini cut an unforgettable dash in those grey and increasingly troubled days in Northern Ireland. On the gleaming red and silver MV Agustas, he blazed a path to glory in the races as well as through the hearts of every Irish woman who saw him!

For the record, Agostini scored wins at Dundrod in both 1969 and 1970 when these pictures were taken. They were comparatively easy victories as both he and the MV machines were superior to the rest of the opposition at the time. So superior that even when his 350cc three-cylinder bike went on to two cylinders for the final three laps he still beat second place man Heinz Rosner by over two minutes!

CLIFFORD McLEAN

CLIFFORD McLEAN

Mike Hailwood is making history in this photograph.

The lap record of 108.77mph he set in the 1967 Senior TT on the 500cc Honda 4 would stand until 1975 when Mick Grant set a new record speed. Riding a bike 250cc bigger and with eight years of development in equipment such as disc brakes and slick tyres, Grant managed at last to lay to rest the ghost of Hailwood's legacy.

Nothing divides motorcycle racing fans like the argument as to who was the greatest road racer of them all. With none of the recent crop of world champions like Roberts, Rainey, Lawson, Doohan or Rossi ever racing over pure road courses, the discussion has largely got bogged down in the past when the Grands Prix season included road circuits. Much else has changed and there is no comparison between a champion like Valentino Rossi who races one bike over twenty-five laps of a purpose-built track, and a man like Mike Hailwood, who would compete on both closed public roads and short circuits and in several races in one day on a variety of machinery.

Today's champions appear burnt-out by the time they are thirty. Having retired from bikes to try four-wheel racing, Hailwood decided in 1978, at the age of thirty-eight, to return to the TT. His comeback win, against all the odds, surely marks him out as a champion without peer.

hailwood

british legend

How many men are instantly recognised by only their first names? Joey and wee Robert, the Dunlop brothers, are names that have had an unbroken association with road racing over the last thirty years.

Many people thought they were very different characters – Joey quiet and shy, Robert more publicity conscious and outgoing, but I am not so sure that there is such a difference. Watching the pair of them at work you could see the same style and manner. They shared the same studied approach, modest but unbowed in their self-belief, and God help the person who makes an approach at the wrong time, moments before a race, or when a meticulous piece of engine work is being finished off!

Perhaps the most obvious Dunlop trait is their determination to succeed. This always increased when failure appeared certain. Down the years fans and fellow racers alike have thought to their cost that the wee men were a spent force, only to see the famous yellow or black and white helmets take the chequered flag yet again.

In a world of multi-million-pound race teams and full-time mechanics, the Dunlops always had a hands-on approach, doing most of the mechanical work themselves. That they were as interesting to photograph away from the racetrack as they were on it has been a great attraction for me. Some of my favourite photographs of the brothers have been taken away from the limelight – although at times I have been so engrossed in watching and listening to them that I almost forgot to take any pictures at all!

the dunlops
joey and robert

Robert in 1990

STEPHEN DAVISON

No ordinary Joe

A youthful Joey in 1982.
Or is that just Joe?

making her ready

Joey at work on his 250cc Honda in the paddock
at the 1994 Tandragee 100

the shed

Robert at work on his 125cc Honda race engine
in the shed at his Ballymoney home

STEPHEN DAVISON

prancing horse

fairy tale win

STEPHEN DAVISON

side by side

The Dunlop brothers at the 'Magic Roundabout' during the 1991 North West 200

the pudding basins

blindly led

Determination is written all over the face of sidecar driver Siegfried Schauzu as he steers his **BMW** outfit out of the Gooseneck on his way to victory in the 1969 750cc Sidecar TT.

Passenger Horst Schneider on the other hand has no idea where he is going given that his goggles are completely covering his eyes. They do say you have to be a bit mad to be a sidecar passenger – perhaps it helps if you can't see too!

One of the most famous rivalries in world road racing spilled on to the Irish roads in 1968 when team-mates Bill Ivy and Phil Read brought their 'works' Yamahas to Dundrod for the Ulster Grand Prix.

Read had already won the 125cc world championship and the Yamaha race bosses had issued team orders that he should assist Ivy in clinching the 250cc title. But the irascible Read declared he would not follow the orders and set about trying to do the double.

Speculation over the cut-and-thrust 250cc battle brought more than ninety thousand spectators to the Dundrod circuit, packed along the hedgerows. The Yamaha pair didn't disappoint, swapping the lead lap after lap until fate eventually intervened and a stone holed Read's radiator, forcing his retirement and giving Ivy an easy win. As one motorcycling paper reported, the diminutive Ivy obviously had friends among the 'little people' of Ireland!

wasps in a jam jar

Van Veen Kriedler, Jamathi and Derbi – not names you would readily associate with a grey Dundrod day at the Ulster Grand Prix in 1970!

Jan Schrugers (5), Angel Nieto (1), Alt Toerson (3), Martin Mijwaart (7) and Jan de Vries (4) lined up for evening practice on the exotic tiny 50cc machines that formed one of the Grand Prix world championship classes in the sixties and seventies.

Incredibly, Angel Nieto, the second most successful Grand Prix champion in history after Giacomo Agostini, took his Derbi to a race win at an average speed of 82.40mph. Just imagine flying down the Deer's Leap at over 100mph on a machine no bigger than a push-bike!

ROWLAND WHITE

ROWLAND WHITE

zipping past

A rare appearance by
Phil Read at the North West
in 1969 was marked by some
difficulties with his race kit.

Brilliantly captured by Rowland White as he
was forced to make some running repairs to his
leathers during the race, Read managed to hold
on to second place on his Yamaha behind Rod
Gould throughout the 350cc race – despite the
distraction!

end of an era

A wonderfully evocative shot by Rowland White of the 500cc grid lined up for practice in Portstewart at the 1971 North West 200. Rowland worked as a photographer for *Motorcycling* magazine throughout the sixties and seventies, witnessing enormous changes in racing and photography along the way.

Today the North West start line and pits are further out along the Coast Road towards Portrush, with the big teams arriving in massive transporters complete with hospitality areas. In 1971, a racer was more likely to arrive in a Transit van complete with mattress and kettle!

Shooting this picture, Rowland was armed with a Rolleiflex camera that only allowed a dozen shots per roll of film. Today he shoots with a digital camera and memory cards, storing hundreds of images on each one.

Interestingly, almost all the bikes in this shot are British and four-stroke but within a couple of years two-stroke Japanese machinery would dominate such a scene.

Amongst those ready for the off are Harris Healy (65), Jack McAfee (62), Charlie Dobson (57), Sam McClements (66), Bill Smith (53), Gerry Mateer (56), Geoff Barry (97), M. Begley (90), Harry Turner (95), Ken Turner (23), Chas Dunlop (93), Steve Murray (26) and Alex George (27).

down at the seaside
north west 200

elbow to elbow

This picture sums up the difference between Irish road racing and the Isle of Man TT.

At the TT it is the rider against the course and the clock, each racer leaving the line individually at ten-second intervals. In Ireland it is mass start racing, rider against rider, all hurtling into that first corner looking for the precise piece of Tarmac that Michael Rutter occupies here during the 2003 North West 200.

dhu varren

A scene never to be repeated!

This would simply not be permitted in today's safety conscious environment. Fans cover every inch of the bridge and banking at Dhu Varren in Portrush for a view of the 250cc race at the 1970 North West 200. The spectators on the bridge are actually standing on the railway track – apart from those who are hanging off the bridge itself! When a train came along the driver had to crawl to walking speed and blow the whistle as people moved out of the way.

There is hardly a space to be found on the Metropole railway embankment as Mick Grant sweeps the 750cc Kawasaki up to Church in the 1977 North West 200.

GAVAN CALDWELL

Mick Grant on the North West 200 grid in 1977

ROWLAND WHITE

mick grant
green meanie

The famous 'Green Meanie' Kawasaki machines ridden by Mick Grant and Barry Ditchburn became one of the most famous race teams of the seventies. Unlike Barry Sheene, his great rival in Britain at this time, Grant was always keen to race at the TT and on the Irish roads, and he became a huge favourite with the fans.

father . . .

A specialist on the smaller two-stroke 250cc and 350cc machines, Tony Rutter was a regular double race winner in these categories on the Irish roads.

Little wonder then that the fans would seek out any vantage point on the North West 200's Coast Road section to get a glimpse of the famous TR helmet in full flight. Unfortunately, on this wet Saturday in 1974, Tony had to settle for second on his Yamaha in the 350cc class, behind that other dominant Englishman of the 1970s, John Williams.

. . . and son

Knee grinding the road as he enters the start and finish chicane on a Ducati in 2003, Michael Rutter has followed his father Tony on to the North West roads and is now only one race win short of his dad's total of nine.

eddie laycock

The crowd crane their necks to watch Eddie Laycock scream the Team Millar-liveried Honda into Millbank corner during the 1990 North West 200.

Over the last thirty years racers from Northern Ireland have dominated the Irish road racing scene with one exception –

STEPHEN DAVISON

Carl Fogarty had been trying to win a race at the North West 200 for half a dozen years, often leading, but either breaking down or crashing with the chequered flag in sight.

How much a North West victory meant to the man who became the most famous bike racer in Britain is obvious by his reaction when he

finally achieved his goal in 1993. Stepping off the Moto Cinelli 888 Ducati he raised his hands to the heavens in thanks for the divine intervention that he felt had made his win possible at last. A couple of hours later he broke the lap record to make it two wins in a day on the Triangle course.

43

With concentration etched across his face, Iain Duffus leads a fiercely contested feature race into the final corner at the North West 200 in 2002.

Adrian Archibald, tucked in behind, dived around the outside and the two men crossed the line side by side. Onlookers couldn't tell the two apart and initially Archibald was declared the winner.

Closer examination by the line judges gave the victory to Duffus, though even today the television replay appears inconclusive.

iain duffus
neck and neck

brian steenson

Brian Steenson (121) lets it all hang out as he leads Tommy Robb through Henry's corner in the 500cc race at the 1970 North West 200. In spite of his unorthodox style, Steenson set the fastest lap of the day at over 108mph.

With his tousled mop and daredevil style, Brian Steenson made a huge and immediate impact on the Irish road racing scene at the end of the sixties. Miss *Motorcycle News*, Louise Duffin, was obviously impressed by his charms!

Sadly Steenson's rise to fame was cut cruelly short at just twenty-three years of age when he was killed in a crash at the Senior TT the following year.

the ultimate price

john williams

CLIFFORD McLEAN

Long before I was a photographer, I was a fan of road racing. One of my favourite memories is of sitting under the trees at Cochranstown on a sunny Saturday afternoon as John Williams blasted his way up the leafy green tunnel. As he flew past and up into the fast approach to Quarterlands, my Uncle Johnny, who took me to all the races in those days, jumped to his feet and shouted, 'Ah Jaysus boys, that's delightful cornering.' Not much moved my Uncle Johnny to use a word like delightful but the style of John Williams en route to another Dundrod victory was a sight demanding such flowery language.

The Ulster Grand Prix of 1978 was the last year we would witness such a spectacle. The day started well for Williams with a start to finish win in the 500cc race and this podium celebration. Rounding Wheeler's corner in this photograph Williams was on his way to fourth place in the Formula One race.

Only a few minutes later, in the 1000cc event, he lost control of his 750cc Yamaha, crashing at this very same spot. Initially it seemed Williams had suffered no more than a broken collarbone as he walked to the ambulance and joked with the crowd, but later that night he died as a result of the injuries he had sustained.

47

tom herron
seconds from death

BILLY REID

Tom Herron could have had no thought of what awaited him when this picture was taken as he sped along the Coast Road between Portrush and Portstewart on Saturday 25 May, 1979. He was only seconds from death.

The headline in the Belfast newspapers the next morning read 'Black Saturday'. Two riders died on Irish road racing's most dreadful day and a third, Armoy Armada racer, Frank Kennedy, died later as a result of injuries sustained in a high-speed crash.

As is so often the case, the death of the second racer, the relatively unknown nineteen-year-old Brian Hamilton from Scotland, was completely overshadowed by the headlines given to the death of Tom Herron, Ireland's biggest road racing star.

Herron had been the most successful privateer in the Grand Prix world championship series over the previous couple of seasons and his reward had been a contract to race 500cc Grand Prix 'works' bikes alongside former world champion Barry Sheene in the Suzuki team.

Indeed, in the early part of the season, Tom had outshone his illustrious team-mate until a crash at the Spanish Grand Prix the week before the North West left him with a damaged right hand. The strapping on it can be seen in this picture.

The debate has raged ever since as to whether or not Herron was fit to ride the fearsome 652cc Suzuki superbike machine. Whatever the answer, with the world seemingly at his feet, his luck ran out on the final lap of the last race of the day at Juniper Hill.

DEREK McINTYRE

Although twenty years separate these two photographs, they are linked by a common thread.

In both pictures the mercurial Joey Dunlop is battling with a respected but bitter rival at Temple jumps. In 1977, when the first of these pictures was taken, Joey's career was only beginning and Raymond McCullough was the target man at the top of the pile. The picture has become one of the most famous road racing photographs of all time as it was used to publicise the award-winning film, *The Road Racers*, which documented the careers of the Armoy Armada.

By 1997, Joey was the man to beat and Owen McNally was the new rising star. Tragically both Joey and Owen were to die within a year of each other in racing crashes. Owen was leading the 250cc race at the 1999 Ulster Grand Prix when he was killed at Dawson's bend and Joey lost his life in Estonia the following year.

DEREK McINTYRE

temple jumps

Legendary Irish bike racing photographer Derek McIntyre is the man behind both images. Derek practically discovered Temple jumps as a photographic location and made them his own over the years. An old friend of Joey Dunlop, Derek travelled the world with the Ballymoney man during his years of racing in the Formula One world championship.

gary jess
alexander's leap

The late Gary Alexander Jess rises up out of the seat to jump the famous Alexander's Leap during the 2002 Mid-Antrim 150. On the brink of major success, Gary lost his life in 2002 in a crash at Cochranstown corner during the Ulster Grand Prix.

STEPHEN DAVISON

ISLE OF MAN
G CAPITAL OF THE WORLD
1999

1999
I.O.M. T.T.
ULTRA L/WEIGHT
THIRD

1999
I.O.M. T.T.
ULTRA L/WEIGHT
SECOND

ULTRA LIGHT
THIRD

ULTRA LIGHTWEIGHT
SECOND 1999

STEPHEN DAVISON

dynes & mcnally
brothers-in-arms

Friendly rivals!

After battling for 150 miles over the toughest racecourse
in the world, Gary Dynes and Owen McNally share a
special moment after the 1999 Ultra-Lightweight TT.
Little more than a year after this picture was taken both
men were killed in separate racing accidents.

53

david jefferies
simply the best

I was sitting on top of the Isle of Man
TT's mountain road when I heard that
David Jefferies was dead.

It would have been stunning news at any time but given that I
had just photographed him a few minutes before, it was
impossible to grasp. The roar of his engine had drowned out the
mountain wind as he flicked the big Suzuki from right to left
through the sweeping twists of Keppel Gate. We waited as word
drifted through to fill the silence that followed. DJ had been
killed a few miles down the road, crashing at Crosby on his
second practice lap. He never made it back to Keppel Gate.

The record books highlight a remarkable career: North West
and Ulster Grand Prix wins, short-circuit championships and,
most impressive of all, three trebles at the TT in consecutive
years. David Jefferies was the fastest man ever around the
37.75-mile TT course at 127.29mph. No-one has ever achieved
so much in the ultimate motorcycle racing challenge in such a
short space of time.

Of course, bad news is no stranger to road racing and the
fastest men are those in the greatest danger. But that does not
make it any easier to accept what has happened. There is still a
part of us all waiting to see DJ again on that second lap.

billy reid *photographer*

Billy Reid

was only ten years old when his father took him to the 1952 Ulster Grand Prix on the old Clady course. Almost instantly the motorbike bug bit hard.

Initially he was happy as a spectator, but when road racing really took off in the seventies, Billy was inspired to take up the camera. That decade saw a big boost in the sport in Ireland with the birth of the legendary Armoy Armada (Joey and Jim Dunlop, Mervyn Robinson and Frank Kennedy) and their adversaries, the Dromara Destroyers (Raymond McCullough, Brian Reid and Trevor Steele), alongside a host of other local talents like Ian McGregor, Abe Alexander, Billy Guthrie and Courtney Junk.

The most remarkable thing is the quality of Billy's coverage given the limited nature of his camera kit. A Russian-made Zenith E, bought second-hand for £25, a standard 50mm lens and a 200mm f4 Meyer lens were hardly state of the art even then and compared to today's multi-thousand-pound

all-singing, all-dancing cameras it is almost laughable.

Money was in short supply and Billy never made any fortune. 'I got a couple of quid from the *Ballymena Guardian* every few years!' he remembers. But Billy proved it was the eye behind the camera that really mattered and coupled with a wonderful ability to get into places other photographers never even thought of, he has produced a unique record of the seventies.

He laughs off the problems in his typically modest way. 'I knew I could get pictures easily at the slow hairpins but I wanted something different, a harder challenge. I didn't get many sharp but when I did they were different.'

Surprisingly, he rarely attends races today. 'I just got fed up arguing with marshals about where I could photograph from and I decided to hang up the cameras and go fishing on a Saturday,' he explains.

For the last twenty years his negatives have been gathering dust in his attic. Until now. Enjoy a step back in time to an era when every grid was covered in a cloud of blue smoke and every racer seemed to be doused in the oil that created it!

What goes up must come down! Joey Dunlop tortures his front tyre on landing at the Temple jumps in 1978.

BILLY REID

north west '79
the blue haze

BILLY REID

A blue haze of two-stroke smoke hangs over
the North West 200 grid in 1979 as the crowds
throng the Coast Road at Portstewart.

John Williams (3) blasts off the line on his Yamaha in the 1973 350cc race at the Ulster Grand Prix to make the day the 'John Williams Show'.

The Cheshire racer followed up his 350cc victory with wins in the 250cc and 500cc events to become the first rider in the forty-four-year history of the 'Ulster' to score a treble.

This evocative Clifford McLean picture captures Williams leaving some famous names in his wake: Charlie Williams (1), Abe Alexander (44), Ian McGregor (33), Tom Herron (29), Mick Grant (8), Phil Carpenter (4), Campbell Gorman (38) and Billy Guthrie (6) are amongst the pursuing pack.

ulster grand prix 1973

CLIFFORD McLEAN

the armoy armada

In 1977 a supporters' club was set up to help finance the racing of north Antrim men Mervyn Robinson, Joey and Jim Dunlop, and Frank Kennedy, the now legendary Armoy Armada. Attracting a huge and fanatically loyal following, their appearance boosted local interest in road racing as they did battle with the Dromara Destroyers, led by Raymond McCullough. Tragically, Frank Kennedy (1979) and Mervyn Robinson (1980) were killed in crashes at the North West 200, leading to the disbandment of the club.

Jim Dunlop, the only surviving member of the Armoy Armada

BILLY REID

Joey and Mervyn share a smile and some body language in the Tandragee paddock in 1978.

BILLY REID

Shoulder to shoulder, Joey Dunlop and Mervyn Robinson prepare to push-start off the line at the 1975 Mid-Antrim 150.

Gavan Caldwell, the man behind this rare colour image, was working as an amateur photographer in those early days. He is now a full-time professional photographer and a permanent fixture in the race paddocks.

BILLY REID

Transit vans, duffle coats and Big Frank Kennedy, the third man in the Armoy Armada line-up

63

cloughwater bridge

There's not an inch of rubber on the Tarmac as Joey Dunlop leads Noel Hudson over the narrow Cloughwater Bridge at the Mid-Antrim 150 in 1980.

A rare and glorious colour shot of Sam McClements flying the famous Ryan Norton over the Temple jumps in 1977. The Ryan Norton never won any *concours d'élégance* awards but it did win plenty of races!

sam's the man

Tom Herron in the 500cc race at Quarry bends during the Ulster Grand Prix, 1978. Now that's what I call a race crowd!

BILLY REID

seventies scrapbook

For those of us lucky enough to have been there, the seventies are fondly remembered as the heyday of road racing. Groovy clothes and dodgy hairstyles brightened the huge crowds and the full race grids. Their look might appear a bit strange now but guys like Ron Haslam and Percy Tait were the kings of the road – rockstar racers! These pictures brilliantly capture the spirit of those paddocks.

BILLY REID

A wild man

Superstar of the 1970s racing scene, **Percy Tait** poses with an admirer at the North West 200.

What is it that transfixes grown men as they stand around a revving motorcycle?

Stan Woods' RG500 Suzuki is warmed up in front of an appreciative audience in the North West paddock in 1977.

BILLY REID

John Rea and **Hector Neill** – two of the famous names in road racing sponsorship. Their support has launched dozens of careers.

he sea breeze plays havoc with **Tony Rutter's** coiffure on the grid at the 1977 North West 200.

GAVAN CALDWELL

BILLY REID

To the victor the spoils!
Donny Robinson enjoys a congratulatory kiss after an Ulster Grand Prix win.

Mutton chop sideburns were all the rage in the mid-seventies you know! **Ron Haslam** gets the laurels and congratulations from race sponsor Terence McKeag after a Killinchy 150 race win in 1977.

BILLY REID

71

This picture lays to rest an argument that has raged for nearly thirty years. Did Ireland's Tom Herron beat the South African Alan North in the 1977 250cc race at the Ulster Grand Prix or did local bias tip the balance in Herron's favour?

close call

Both riders were credited with the same time and speed but the line judges declared the Ulsterman the winner.

Previously unpublished, this picture shows that Herron (3) has a definite advantage over North as they dash for the line.

BILLY REID

supermac

Phillip McCallen
moments before the race start
at the 1993 North West 200

Mr TT

Often styled the Prince of the Roads to Joey Dunlop's King, Phillip McCallen became the dominant force in road racing in the 1990s.

Winner of eleven TTs, who would have thought on the day this picture was taken, at Quarterbridge in the 1997 Senior TT, that it would be the last time we would see him win on the island? This victory completed a unique achievement – four TT wins in one week, a feat not equalled before or since.

Unfortunately, injury resulting from a series of high-speed crashes forced a premature end to a brilliant career two years later.

STEPHEN DAVISON

STEPHEN DAVISON

gladiator

With sweat glistening on his brow, Phillip McCallen exudes a gladiatorial pride as he defies the opposition to better his practice time at the 1997 Ulster Grand Prix.

under a big sky

After a lengthy lay-off through injury, Phillip McCallen made a return to racing in 1999 at the Tandragee 100 in County Armagh. However, his comeback was brief – the injuries he had suffered to his back and shoulder forced his retirement after the TT that year.

Dukes bends

Martin Finnegan

Gillies jump

Tens of thousands of people turn out to sit on the grassy banks at the Skerries road races in County Dublin every year, making it the biggest motorcycling event in the Republic of Ireland.

In 2003 they were able to cheer local hero Martin Finnegan (far left) to a home win.

Recently, a new ruling by the Motorcycle Union of Ireland, the body that governs bike racing in Ireland, requires races to set aside a separate period for practice. In effect, this means that all races have become two-day meetings.

Race organisers in the North have come up against opposition from residents and business people opposed to two days of road closures, forcing the end of meetings like the Carrowdore 100 and threatening several others. However, in the South local communities have turned the meetings into popular festivals, with new races springing up in the last few years in places like Dundalk, Athea and Faugheen.

the skerries

81

6 a.m.

Early morning TT practice on the
Glencrutchery Road. The marshal's worried
expression says it all. With jangling nerves and
sweaty palms who wants to read about greasy
Tarmac and mud on the road as they are just
about to head down the most terrifying piece
of racing road in the world?

STEPHEN DAVISON

on the island

waterworks

One of the joys of being a road racing
photographer is the working environment.
Jim Moodie follows the flow through the
Waterworks bends during the Isle of Man TT
in 2002.

creg ny baa

Stretching for home!

With Kate's Cottage shining in the sun, Adrian Archibald (13) fends off cramp as he battles with Joey Dunlop (12) and Ronnie Smith (11) at Creg Ny Baa during the 1999 Junior TT.

TT masters

Phillip McCallen, Joey Dunlop (as always in different kit from the rest), **Carl Fogarty, Steve Hislop** and **Graeme McGregor** join team boss Neil Tuxworth for an unofficial photograph of the official Honda line-up at the 1990 TT. Together they have won fifty-three TTs.

Having covered every TT, Manx Grand Prix and Southern 100 since 1983, photographer Dave Purves knew this was a special picture. A former racer himself, Dave lives just a few hundred yards from the TT grandstand.

STEPHEN DAVISON

kiwi triumph

British factory Triumph returned to the TT in 2003 after a long absence, hoping to recapture the glory days when domestic manufacturers dominated on the island.

Their optimism was well founded with Kiwi Bruce Anstey (12) winning the 600cc Junior TT on the Union Jack-liveried bike. Ryan Farquhar (10) had the satisfaction of breaking the lap record as he chased Anstey home past the crowds at the Gooseneck.

the mountain road

STEPHEN DAVISON

A sidecar blasts up the mountain section of the Isle of Man TT course with Ramsey in the background during TT 2002.

welsh wizard

STEPHEN DAVISON

Raindrops covering his visor, Ian Lougher peers out of the gloom.

90

Approached at over 150mph, Ballacrye jump is an incredible place to watch road racing. The bikes take off and fly through the air for fifty or sixty yards. Here, Ian Lougher enjoys the thrill during the 2002 Senior TT.

on the street

Dwarfing his little 125cc machine, **Gary Dynes** seems bound for the parlours of the Ballaugh cottages as he races through the village streets during the 1999 Ultra-Lightweight TT.

STEPHEN DAVISON

You are the man! **David Jefferies** celebrates in the winner's enclosure after being told that he has just become the first man ever to break the 125mph lap record in the 2000 Senior TT.

The sweet taste of success!

John McGuinness catches a mouthful of bubbly after winning the Lightweight TT in 1999.

lougher & jefferies
the little and large show

Ian Lougher shares a joke with
his taller team-mate David
Jefferies as they top the podium
at the 2002 Isle of Man TT.

97

robert dunlop
miracle on wheels

In 1998, Robert Dunlop arrived in the Isle of Man for the TT races on crutches, still suffering from the effects of a horrific accident at the North West 200 a couple of weeks previously.

He was entered for just one race, the Ultra-Lightweight 125cc TT, but most observers felt that he had little chance of making the start line.

That Robert wanted to race a motorbike anywhere at all was (and still is) a source of great wonder to almost everyone in the racing world. He was already severely hampered by the continuing effects of a massive accident during the 1994 TT when his Honda RC45's back wheel collapsed at Ballaugh village, firing him into a stone wall at over 100mph. He survived, but only just, and the damage to his legs and right arm in particular led to concerns and controversy about his ability to race.

For everyone but Robert Dunlop, that is!

Having passed a medical examination on his arrival on the island, Robert set about preparing his little 125cc Honda as meticulously as possible. Perhaps fortuitously his garage was at the home of his physiotherapist, Fiona Gilliland, and so as he built engines and checked suspension she massaged and stretched his battered arms and legs!

Nevertheless, there was no disguising his pain as Robert pulled on the helmet for the opening practice sessions. The 125cc race bikes have a tiny powerband and require thousands of gear changes on every lap of the TT course, torturing tattered collarbones and ankles. The bumpy sections must have seemed like ploughed fields.

Undeterred, Robert soldiered on, determined to at least put on a good show for his legions of fans. Initially he was cagey in front of the cameras, wary of how they were portraying him in his weakened condition. My original request to photograph him receiving treatment for his broken leg at the paddock in the back of the van was refused but when I visited the garage a couple of days later I found him in great spirits, laughing and joking with his helpers between puffs on the obligatory roll-ups. After the bike was rebuilt Robert turned to me and asked where I wanted to take the picture. Not sure what he meant I must have looked puzzled and he pointed to his foot. A few moments later he was having the cast removed and receiving physio in the back garden of the house in front of the camera. Every move he made was big news, but if Robert was under pressure he wasn't showing it.

Race day dawned sunny and dry, a blessing for Robert. I remember talking to his pit crew just before the start and their concern was obvious. The fear was that Robert's determination might lead to a rash chance being taken, a bend approached just a bit faster than before. The TT is extremely unforgiving of moments when the heart, no matter how big, rules the head.

But all the concerns were unfounded. In glorious sunshine
Robert Dunlop scorched to a fantastic fairy tale win.
No-one could match his pace through Glen Helen or
over the Mountain Mile. Skimming the white railings
at Ginger Hall and screaming out of the Gooseneck,
no-one saw the way he went that bright June day.

STEPHEN DAVISON

Old rival Ian Lougher and up-and-coming star Owen McNally shared Robert's pleasure on the podium, though with an air of disbelief that they had been beaten by a man racing with little more than the power of one arm and leg. There were tears of joy and relief in the winner's enclosure and the champagne never tasted so sweet.

STEPHEN DAVISON

105

Gary Dynes has his foot
shaken off the footrest by the
Tandragee bumps as he exits
Castle corner during the
feature race in 1999.

gary dynes
close shave

moments

graeme crosby
southern star

Having already clinched the Formula One world title earlier in the day, flamboyant Australian Graeme Crosby was determined to celebrate his trip to the Ulster Grand Prix at Dundrod in 1980.

He spent most of the Classic race entertaining the huge crowd of ecstatic fans at Leathemstown with an awesome display of wheelies.

Crosby was undoubtedly feeling well disposed to Ulster folk, having benefited from the generosity of his new team-mate, one William Joseph Dunlop Esq., who had been drafted into the Suzuki squad to help Crosby beat the Honda duo of Mick Grant and Ron Haslam in the important Formula One world championship. Grant only had to finish behind Crosby to win the title. Dunlop's task was to

CLIFFORD McLEAN

finish between the pair, ensuring Suzuki would win the title.

Joey did just that but made his point along the way, blasting into a twenty-second lead before slowing with a 'misfire' to let Haslam win and Crosby through, keeping his own machine ahead of Grant.

Dunlop's ride and Crosby's wheelie celebrations around the Dundrod course are now part of Irish road racing legend but on the day the race organisers were less than impressed with the Australian's antics and he got a ticking off from the clerk of the course!

109

archibald and iris

miaoooooooow!

Cat lover Pamela Shaw felt sure
her beloved Iris was happily
snoozing on her favourite chair . . .

It was only when she opened the *Ballymena Times* a
week later that she realised that Iris had spent the
evening dicing with death as the motorbikes blasted
through their home village of Clough in County
Antrim during the Mid-Antrim 150's practice session
in 2000.

Times photographer John McIlwaine was lying against
a straw bale contemplating the miseries of the Friday
evening shift when he spotted the cat tearing across
the road as Adrian Archibald exited the chicane. 'I
managed to get the camera to my eye and fired off a
few frames as Iris scooted across the track,' he recalls.

One life gone, eight to go!

JOHN McILWAINE

A titanic battle of the tiddlers!

You could almost cover the trio of Owen McNally (37), Denis McCullough (4) and Robert Dunlop (40) with a handkerchief as they hurtle over the jumps on their 125cc bikes during the Carrowdore 100 in 1997.

tiny trio

sunshine and showers

With both wheels pawing the air, Ryan Farquhar jumps through Farmhouse corner in bright sunshine during the 2003 Cookstown 100. Moments later Alex Donaldson struggles to find his way around the course as the rain dances off the road.

hislop crashes
north west 1988

This amazing shot of Steve Hislop crashing his RVF 750cc Honda at Church corner in the 1988 North West 200 Production Race is from the archives of Clifford McLean.

Look closely and you can see pieces of the bike literally disintegrating in front of your eyes. The back wheel is twisted and fuel is escaping from the tank. Happily, Hislop was unhurt but the bike and straw bales went up in flames. Incredibly, this photograph has never been published before.

This is perhaps understandable given the vast McLean archive – it is easy to miss one picture when you have tens of thousands taken over a forty-year career of shooting bikes. Hailing from Ballymoney, the County Antrim town which has become synonymous with road racing, Clifford has built up a huge collection of images which includes everyone who has graced the roads of Ireland on a racing motorbike.

117

hedge cutter

You almost feel you could throw your leg over the hedge and jump on board with Adrian Archibald for a high-speed lap of Dundrod.

Ulster Grand Prix, 2002

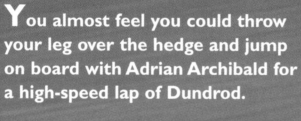

big air

For ordinary Glaslough traffic, on the 364 days of the year when the Monaghan road races are not taking place, the rise in the road at Cassidy's sawmill is just a bit of a bump. On that other day it is a ramp into the unknown for Richard Britton!

heading for home

Darren Burns steers his little 125cc Honda around the thick hedges that line the Glaslough course in County Monaghan in 2002.

123

the final bend

Adrian Archibald lays on an awesome demonstration in high-speed cornering at Quarry bends during the 2003 Dundrod 150 races.

Every few years a new figure rises up to dominate the road racing scene. In 2003 that man has been Adrian Archibald. Overcoming the tragic loss of his team-mate David Jefferies at TT 2003, Archibald won both the Formula One and Senior races to secure his place at the top.

No motorcycle racing photograph has ever frozen a moment in time so precisely as this shot of the dead heat finish in the 350cc race at the 1977 North West 200.

The crowd look on open-mouthed, the line judge strains to watch the wheels cross the line, and the chequered flag is poised waiting to drop. You can almost hear the silence as the moment hangs suspended in time forever.

Irish legend Raymond McCullough (1) and English stalwart Tony Rutter (6), both on Yamahas, were part of a six-strong group that had battled throughout the race. McCullough eventually

the flag drops . . . .

made the break and opened a slight gap, but going into the final corner he made a mistake and Rutter got the better drive to the line. Did Rutter just nick it?

Whatever the verdict, it is another one of those unforgettable moments that road racing has produced down the years. As fans we all have our favourite memories of wonderful races and riders from the past, a past that often seems more golden than the present. There is no doubt that road racing faces more difficult challenges today than ever before and it is tempting to avoid them by looking backwards. The challenges will have to be met, but while there are men (and the occasional woman) who want to race the roads, and fans who want to watch them, road racing will live on.

AFTER ALL, WHAT ELSE IS THE SUMMER FOR?

Acknowledgements

Very special thanks are due to Damian Keenan for nurturing the idea of this book, to Leslie Moore for guiding its direction, and to Wendy Dunbar, Patsy Horton and Bronagh McVeigh at Blackstaff Press for giving it form and shape. I am also grateful to my colleagues at Pacemaker Press International for their support throughout the project.

Thanks too go to Billy Reid, Clifford McLean, Rowland White, Derek McIntyre, Gavan Caldwell and Dave Purves for granting permission for their photographs to be used.

Every effort has been made to trace and contact copyright holders before publication. If notified, the publisher will rectify any errors or omissions at the earliest opportunity.

First published in October 2003 by
Blackstaff Press Limited
4c Heron Wharf, Sydenham Business Park
Belfast BT3 9LE, Northern Ireland

Reprinted November 2003

Printed in England by The Bath Press

A CIP catalogue record for this book is available from the British Library

ISBN 0-85640-747-X

www.blackstaffpress.com